Black Man Raise Your Children!

By Linda D. Crowder

Dedicated to Marion Crowder, my uncle for whom I am forever grateful. I would never have written this book if you hadn't told to me to "Put it in a book!"

Thank you.

Preface

This not a book to be read from cover to cover for entertainment purposes; but, to be read one chapter at a time: "Meditate on these things".

If I could reach one...then I will teach one. I would teach him the errors of his ways. I would teach him not to make the same mistakes that I made. I would give him my life on a silver platter so that his platter could turn to pure gold. Linda D. Crowder

TABLE OF CONTENTS

I Timothy 5:8

But if any provide not for his own, and specially for those of his own house, he has denied the faith, and is worse than an infidel.

1. Provide for your children
2. Those of your seed
3. If you do not, then you have denied the faith. What faith? The faith in which you say you believe in....
4. You are worse than an unbeliever.

Do You Know Who You Are? Know Yourself.

Genesis 50:11

And when the inhabitants of the land, the Canaanites, saw the mourning in the floor of Atad, they said, this is a grievous mourning to the Egyptians.

The Hebrews were mistaken for the Egyptians....We are the Children of God; therefore, we must wake up and see ourselves and our children for who they are for it is our duty.

In our reawakening of who the black man is and where we came from...we must spring forward and pass this information on to our children. We must build our children up to the giants that they are and were meant to be. We are co-creators with the Almighty...! God allows us to create within His creation. When you look into your child's eyes you should see Almighty God Himself! He's at work in you and He is at work within that child. And when that child looks into our eyes...that child should see God Almighty in you and they do. There is no love like a child's love for his/her parents.

We can ask many questions about God....we can ask God many questions of why...but, there is one thing that we cannot do...WE, THE HUMAN RACE, CANNOT DENY HIS POWER....WE CANNOT DENY THE EXISTENCE OF GOD, WE CANNOT DENY THAT HIGHER, MICRALOUS POWER....WE CANNOT DENY!

When a baby is born, it is born by the miracle working power of Almighty God and not solely because of human intimacy with each other. Therefore, we are to love, protect, and nurture what is born of and created by God Almighty!

CHAPTER 1

RAISE YOUR OWN CHILDREN

I truly believe that God made man first...to lead. How does a man lead? By example. A man leads by his actions. Man is to be good to his seed. Be good to your children for just like a plant or flower you can either destroy them or fertilize, till, and cause them to grow into such beautiful productive human beings, who will give back to God, you, and the world one hundred percent.

God made man in His own image; therefore, our children are created in our image and should be loved and cared for as God loves us. He never left us alone so why should we leave our poor innocent children alone? Alone to grow up in a heartless world, with no guidance or instructions to hold their spirits in place to be prepared for the journey of life.

How sweet it is to hold a new born baby and to feel the love and joy that it gives. How can you deny such an existence of yourself? When I looked into my baby's eyes and heard their first cry...I was mystified! This baby is worth all the pain that I had gone through to bring him/her here. Oh, the joy that flooded my heart. This baby is our miracle from the Almighty. I am thankful, I am blessed. In these arms of mine will I carry this child.

A man is to love, nurture, and care for his children from birth until the end of life. How does one began to raise a child? You raise a child by being the child's provider;

making sure that you have an income to support a child with food, shelter, and clothing. Your source of income should be legal. A man raises his own children by being in their lives daily...changing pampers, combing hair, bathing, and all the other task that comes with daily living. Life happens; therefore, every man cannot be with their children daily in the same home. The next step is to make sure that you make plans to stick to that child like super glue. This will consist of making sure that you have equal time with your child...going to the daycare center, going to the school to volunteer and spend time with them. Your job is to be a part of every aspect of that child's life. Raise your own child/children. This is your responsibility. This is your ultimate duty outside of everything else in life. Your professional career is not your child; but, your child is YOUR career.

You're responsible for giving your children love, morals, and spiritual guidance....not the government, police, or school system. You are your children's first teachers. We are human so we're imperfect; but, your presence and your guidance for your own children makes the difference in their lives. Sometimes, it is even the major factor as to what they end up becoming in life. Such as a doctor, lawyer, or regular law abiding citizen.

Yes, I acknowledge that there are forces outside ourselves that stand in united allegiance against us; but, I dare to tell you on the flip side of the coin you're your own worst enemy when you fail to take care of your own responsibilities. When a man fails to honor his oneness with the Infinite, then he suffers repercussions in many ways and from different sources. If man honors God, then he will honor himself and that extension of himself because he knows that the extension of himself is priceless....all the money in the world cannot pay for the oneness of love. Love unifies. Love sets free. Love builds up. Love tares down those things that needs to be torn down or done away with. See Love is what it is....ACTION! Love is raising your own children.

CHAPTER 2

CHARITY/LOVE

"Love begins at home, and it is not how much we do... but how much love we put in that action". Mother Teresa.

Charity begins within and spreads outward. Love begins within one's own heart and flows out to his children, family, and friends. How can a man say that he loves himself and not love his children? How would you feel or how did you feel abandoned as a child? This is your own flesh and blood, you made this child. In the beginning God created the world and in Genesis God said, "Let us make man in our own image... Do you know who you are and what that means?....and gave him dominion"... you must give your children dominion over their lives...over good and evil. How? You give your children dominion by being the dominant force in their everyday lives. You give to them what our forefathers gave to the world....teach them math, writing, reading or put them in a place of higher learning where they can learn the sciences.

I was taught that "Love is better felt than told". You see because love is an action word. Love is always doing something. Love never stops. Love is tolerance.

The Greatest Gift that you can give your children is Love. Love is not a mere emotion. Love is an action word. Love will cause you to take them to school. Love will move you to help with their homework or either hire someone to tutor them. Love will cause you to lead your children in the path of righteousness for His name sake. Love will cause you to honor that which the Lord has given you. A loved child will be a more productive child/citizen.

You're the protector of your children. The word “Protect” also means to assist and defend.

Stay with them and teach them the ways of this world. How can you do this? By knowing who they are with and where they are at all times. Do not leave your children alone to raise themselves.

Prison...you're responsible for raising your children and keeping them out of prison. At the end of the day you must know in your heart that you've done everything to make this possible.

You must shape your own child's identity and not let the world shape it for them.

CHAPTER 3

LEGITIMATION -KNOW YOUR RIGHTS

(*Disclaimer: I am not an attorney and therefore, cannot give legal advice. I am just sharing my opinion on what I've read and researched online.)

What is Legitimation? Legitimation is the legal process by which a father of a child born outside of marriage becomes the child's legal father which entitles the child to all of the benefits from that father as he or she would have been had the father been married to the mother at the time of the child's birth. The father is responsible for providing support to the child and the child is entitled to inherit from the father. Legitimation also gives the father the right to inherit from the child and to petition the court for child custody and visitation rights.

In Georgia, first look at the law (online). The Official Code of Georgia Annotated (OCGA) is the written collection of the laws of the State of Georgia. The sections for legitimation of a child are OCGA 19-7-20 through OCGA 19-7-27.

A father must not let the fact that he may have to pay child support deter him from establishing his legal rights; because the benefits of legitimizing your children outweigh the money that you have to pay. You may not have to pay as much as you think because you will have to complete a financial affidavit form that details your bills and what you have to pay out. Also, the mother's income may be considered.

Responsible men must open up their eyes and assert their legal rights to their children. You have the right to:

1. Educate yourself on the subject of legitimation.
2. Know the importance of legitimation.
3. Consult an attorney if you don't understand the process.
4. Consult an attorney if you don't know how to go to a website, download the forms, print forms, fill out your name, child's information, and mother's name and address. Go to the courthouse find the right court to file in, pay filing fee, and go before the judge.
    a. Fulton County Family Law website (www.fultoncourt.org)
    b. http://www.albany.ga.us/content/1800/2889/3011/3518/default.aspx
5. Learn your state and local laws on the subject of legitimation.
6. Contact the Office of Child Support Enforcement to inquire about their services.

So many women play the "control" game with their children's father. The mother uses the kids to control the man. You can only see the children when "I" say you can see the children. Our common law system disagrees with this concept. In some jurisdictions, paying child support is not the single factor in determining whether the father gets to see his children.

There is a remedy. The remedy is called “Legitimation – Know Your Rights”. You should study to learn what those rights are. Legitimation provides for court ordered child support and visitation rights and if a person disobeys the court order then they can be held in “contempt”. Google these words “Held in Contempt”.

CHAPTER 4

HOW CAN YOU FORGET ABOUT YOUR OWN CHILDREN?

No one should have to beg you to love your children. Love is automatic. Love rules; therefore, I question your love for your children.

How can you leave your helpless children to move in with another woman and her kids; leaving your precious kids in someone else's hand..Let's talk.

Sit back, close your eyes and do one of two things, remember when you was a child or pretend for a moment that you are a child would you want either one of your parents to **abandon** you? Keep your eyes closed for a second.....can you see yourself taking your first step walking toward your mother or father? Can you see your little self calling out to mommy and daddy? Awwwww, what about your first day at school? Did you cry or feel nervous without your parents being left in a world filled with strangers? Oh, how frightening. Do you remember how you felt when you finally saw your mother or father at the end of the day? I am there with you. I see you. You were so glad to hug and kiss your mom or dad. You slept peacefully that night because you felt safe back at home with your parents. As you dozed off to sleep, their voices calmed your heart and caused you to believe that everything was alright because you were at home. All day long something screamed inside of you, I want mommy or I want daddy. We all want and need our parents that's the way we are made and that is God's order.

Here's the story of Johnny Walker, Jr......

Day after day Little Johnny got off the school bus, he saw many of his friends running home laughing and playing along the way. Johnny wore khaki pants, a white collar shirt with black socks, and basic black tennis shoes. He was ok; not dressed in the best of clothes; but, not too far from the ordinary of the rest of his friends and classmates. He skipped along gleefully as he normally did shouting, “Later man!” to his best buddies as he turned to walk down the path to his own house. He walked inside and threw his purple book bag down heading for the kitchen to see if his blue powerade was where he had hid it the night before.

As he began to drink the cold blue liquid, the deep feeling of “wanting” came over him as it so often did everyday around this time. He wanted his father. He wished for him. He longed for him. He tried to control this aching pain that seemed to go through his whole body; though he knew it was coming from his heart. “I wish dad was here with me every day to help me with my homework or take me fishing or even to just play Nintendo”, he thought to himself.

I love my grandma and my aunty; but, I want daddy. Little Johnny thought about his talk with his friend and best bud Thomas. Thomas had told him that he and his dad had gone to Lake Sinclair fishing on Saturday. Thomas talked about how much fun he had had with his dad and how that when he didn't get a good grade on his spelling test his dad wanted to know why. Thomas had said, “Man, my dad will spank my butt if I don't get all my school work done! My dad is crazy man! Shucks. Every day, he asks me if I need help with my homework or have I done my homework. Sometimes, I will say yes I need help, especially in math when I don't understand Ms. Gragzer. Man, you know how she is! My dad sits down with me and shows me how to do it; but, he be trippin though. Little Johnny often replayed this scene over and over in his mind except that he replaced himself with Thomas and his dad with Thomas' dad. He wanted this to be a reality. To have his dad with him every day. To have his dad get on his butt about his homework. To have his dad "trippin" on him. What did Thomas mean about his dad "trippin"? I'm sure my dad wouldn't be "trippin" like that if he was here with me. Not like Thomas' dad. My dad is cool. As Little Johnny drank the last of the powerade, he threw the bottle in the trash can and a tear went with it. He hurriedly brushed the tear aside, changed out of his school uniform, put on gym shorts and a tee shirt and went outside to play basketball.

What difference could Little Johnny's father have made had he been there for his son? Johnny, Sr. could have asked just a simple question. "Little Johnny, have you done your homework?" Johnny Sr. could have instilled self confidence in his own son. He would have taught him the value of learning and how important it was to the father that the son received a good education and that most of all he took pride in his son and his son's accomplishments; step by step, page by page, grade by grade. Most of all he would have shown his son love. To know that the Father loves you is the greatest love of all in Little Johnny's world.

Instead Little Johnny goes out to play basketball and to chill with his "homies" as usual never experiencing this most important aspect of his life. Little Johnny is with his "boys" in his comfort zone. Learning the language of the streets. Awww, what an awful language it is. Perhaps, this is where he first learns about gang banging, being with the girls, the wrong way to love and live. On the basketball court is where he smelled his first whiff of weed. He eventually tried it and of course liked it. He became a champion, a hero of sorts among his homies. Little Johnny felt comfortable there among his friends; because, many came from the same environment as himself. Hey, they were “good”. Instead of receiving the right education from the right source he received the wrong education from the wrong source. Little Johnny was eventually called in to eat his dinner. His grandmother asked, “Have you done your homework?” “No, Ma'am” “Boy, you better get in there and do your homework!” “Yes, Ma'am. He did his homework; but, hurriedly so. Shall I say more?

Lesson:
When a man does not take responsibility and raise and love his own kids he is saying....
I don't care. I don't care if my child steals, kills, or spend his or her life in and out of prison. I do not love my children. I do not love myself. I am lost. I am dead.

Chapter 5

DON'T LIVE YOUR LIFE AS IF YOUR CHILDREN DON'T EXIST!

Children need the presence of their father even in dire poverty. Do not say that you love your children when you actually don't. There are many fathers who can see their children every day; but, don't. Therefore, putting all of their responsibilities off on someone else. Family members get tired too and sometimes resent you and your carefree lifestyle.

Let's visualize this scenario: Who is responsible for combing or cutting your child's hair? Who is responsible for washing their clothes and giving them a bath? Who should be with them all day and everyday with the exception of school? Who should cook and clean up behind the children?

You are supposed to be a part of your children's lives every day, all day. Don't drop your children off with someone else and pretend as if you have no responsibilities. You leave everybody else to bear the responsibility of your children. Take care of your own children before you take care of someone else's child.

It is insane for a man to leave his own children to go and take care of someone' else's children. How can you call yourself a man? You're not. (1) Your children are your seed. (2) They look up to you. (3) How can you give advice to step children when they see that you're not being responsible with your own children? Let's talk.

Your children are your seed. More likely than not you remember the relationship that you had with their mother. Wild horses couldn't keep you away from this woman. Secondly, perhaps you were right there in the labor and delivery room when the child was born. Oh, such a proud father. You remember all the accolades that you took in...."Congratulations, man!" "Oh, thank you." Remember the late nights? Staying up with the baby? Hearing his/her precious crying? You knew that that child was a miracle. Your eyes were opened to the Omnipotent.

Children look up to their parents; parents are their doctors....their heroes. There isn't anything a parent can't do in the eyes of a child. Would you take this joy away from them intentionally? Would you take this undying love of your child away from yourself? A child's love is pure. It takes a lot of pain to convince a child that their father doesn't care for them.

Many men think that they can give good, constructive advice to their step-children or girlfriend's children. How? People are not ignorant When those children see that you are not taking care of your own responsibility, they are not going to respect you. How can they? For the cycle continues to repeat itself. Those children are missing their own father. Here's another man coming in who is not taking care of his own children, his own responsibility trying to tell them what to do and how to be a man. Man, get out of my face..."You ain't my daddy!" "Man, how are you gonna tell me something?" "You ain't nothing!"

Since you insist on teaching and giving other people kids sound advice, where is the advice for your own children? What is the greatest lesson do you think YOU are teaching them right now? You ARE teaching them that: (1) You don't love them. Love is an action word. Love acts. Love does. You don't love them when you leave them.

Especially, when you can be there in the house with them. You don't love your children when you're not there to get them dressed, to cook and clean for them, to take them to school or pick them up to help them with their homework. You don't love them if you're not there to catch them when they fall or to nurture them in the 101 thousand ways that they need you growing up. Sometimes, just your presence alone makes the difference in their life. You don't care because you're only concerned with doing what you want to do.

The only way to give sound advice and be effective is to first be that responsible person that you are telling that step child to be. When they see your love for yourself, your children and what you do for your own children then and only then can you teach somebody else “how to be”.

CHAPTER 6

THERE IS NOTHING WRONG WITH LIVING WITH YOUR MOTHER

Some people would lead you to believe that there is something wrong with you if you live with your mother past a certain age...I come to tell you that it is all HYPE! Many people do different things at different times in their lives. One of the main reasons is to raise your children. Another reason is to save money for the things you need and want. Most of all, splitting the bills and saving money is cost effective!

There is a lot of misinformation in the world for various reasons. Most of the misinformation is "control propaganda".

Control propaganda comes from those who want the poor to stay poor and the richer to become richer. There is power in numbers. There is power in saving money. There is power in keeping our children out of prison. There is power in knowledge. There is a certain power in knowing that you're not alone and that you do not have to struggle and face each day alone. This power tells you that you CAN and that you WILL!

Control propaganda comes from many venues...some women for example say, "He's a mama's boy!".... to try to make the man feel bad and to feel less than a man. What they are actually saying is...Darn, I can't control you and make you who I want you to be....with your protector around.

Never let another person define who you are. You are a man without anyone's permission.

Raising children demands everything within and out. From birth to adulthood one has constant struggles as well as joys. Staying up all night with their feverish bodies praying that God will heal them. Taking them to the emergency room or staying at the hospital. Focusing on doctor's appointments, food, shelter, and clothing. Sometimes, not knowing where the next meal will come from.

What about when the electrical power is cut off and the house is hot or when the gas is cut off and the child is cold. **Imagine seeing your child's face** when he or she is hungry or cold. School clothes must be provided every year because that is the normal thing to do along with the ever present threat that they can be taken from the parent at any time. Then there's school activities and Christmas to pay for. There is always a "genuine" need for money. The current job is based on education and experience which forces one to go back to school. The sacrifices that a single parent has made can never be compared to any other person.

Let's talk: Every parent wants the best for all of their children and wants them to build and enjoy a better life than what the parent has built. Many people, because of the evil in their hearts sneer at a man that lives with his mother. First, of all that is where he has lived all his life! The relationship is pure and genuine. No tricks or games to be played. No headaches. The experience of life itself causes one to be able to discern the spirit and characteristics of others. Boy, that is a big problem among women. They don't want the mother telling that young man, "Son, she has tricks up her sleeve"! "She doesn't mean you any good, she's all about her self". Many women have preconceived erroneous ideas about what life is all about. An individual is supposed to be an addition to family and not one that comes in to separate a family in the name of love and marriage. Love is what it does. It is action. Love does not separate a man or woman from their mother, children, nor family.

Many women will be the sweetest thing on earth.....have babies and everything until she marries the man and then scream Genesis 2:24 Therefore shall a man leave his father and his mother, and shall cleave unto his wife: and they shall be one flesh. Well, I'm first, I come before your mama, your grandmother, and everybody! What a position to put a man in! He's divided between the two: (1) A mother who has loved and cared for him all his life. (2) a stranger that claims to love him. Why not scream Exodus 20:12 Honor your father and your mother, that your days may be long upon the land which the Lord your God has given you or 1 Corinthians 6:18 (KJV) Flee fornication. Every sin that a man doeth is without the body; but he that committeth fornication sinneth against his own body. Better yet, just don't quote the Bible when you're not a practicing participant.

For an example, a woman will have a job when they first get together: after getting married she will quit her job; because, she thinks that the man should take care of her. This is always feasible when there is a very high income;

but, two incomes are always better than one "low income" household.

Please understand that a lot of men do not come from a two parent home; therefore, Genesis 2:24 may not apply to these men. By the time a single parent raises a child from birth to adulthood they are not rich and may need that child's assistance from time to time. The parent has spent their time, money, and focus on raising their children.

Some, say forget your mother, you're supposed to take care of me. Please don't forget your mother. Your mother didn't forget you. For as long as she needs you until her dying day...be there. Others have accused the mother of wanting her own child for herself. This is by far a great insult; but, they speak from their father the devil. To ask a mother if she wants to have a sexual relationship with her own child, tells that mother that there is something evil in you that is capable of caring out this type of behavior. Evil beyond understanding. Women say that we must start our own family. Yes, that is true; but, that doesn't mean that you're the one for him. It doesn't mean that a man or woman is supposed to forget all about his/her own mother. **When our sons marry the wrong women the family is broken in many different ways.** Many times there is constant friction. Our beliefs are different. Our culture is different. If men would just tell the truth, "I should have listened to my mother"! They wouldn't have gone through the horrifying hell that they did. The reason that women sneer and laugh at a man that lives with his mother is that she can't play all the tricks and follow through on all the devious plans that she has in mind right in front of your mother; because, she knows that mother is watching. The devil don't mind getting you off out there by yourself; because, he can hurt you better and faster. No matter how much you love a person watch them. Watch what they say and do. Watch what they don't say. Does what they say match their actions? Think about your whole life, not just where you are and who you met today. Be yourself and not the person a woman has built up in her mind for you to be to her. Continue to be the loving son, brother, uncle, and family oriented person that you have always been. You will be glad that you did. Don't break up the relationship that you have with your family because nine times out of ten your family is the one that you will be running back to once your eyes has come open to truth.

Why would a loving person want to break up family relationships instead of becoming an integral part of the whole? When one marries into a family that mother-in-law becomes a mother to the daughter-in-law and so does the son-in-law becomes a son to the mother. Thus, the unit of the family is stronger. There isn't anything that I wouldn't do for my sons or daughters. So stop the lies.... Some women boldly state, "I didn't marry the family, I married the man"! No, you marry the family too because the man makes up that family. The family is included in the happiness of their family member. This is the main reason for a BIG celebration whenever there is a marriage.

CHAPTER 7

STAY OUT OF JAIL

Obey the Law....work lawfully and meaningfully to change laws that are not in your best interest or those that you want changed. Introduce new laws that will benefit everybody.

Perhaps, you've heard the saying "Ignorance to the law is no excuse!" Therefore, you must learn from this statement and actually study the law so that you can teach your children the law and not circumvent ways to go around the law; but, live right!

A life of crime isn't really leaving at all! Teach your children the value of being free. Free to go to school. Free to work and play. Introduce them to sports and not the streets.

How to stay out of jail:

1. Don't commit any crimes.
2. Pay your child support. If and when you need help. Get help.
3. Study the Law- Study your state and local laws. Know the law: For an example, many people may "think" that they know what the law is when they really don't. Study the actual words of the law instead of assuming that you know. Know your facts. Never assume anything. Match the facts with the law. For an example: If the law states that 55 mph is the speed limit and you're going 65... then

you're over the speed limit and guilty of breaking that particular law.

4. Leave their poison alone.
5. Don't sell drugs. Sell t-shirts or something. Anything legal. At least by selling t-shirts you will expand your target market.

It is "your" joy and duty to stay clean and out of jail. For this is the rule that your children will learn from you; No matter where you are in life, wake up, stand up, and fulfill your destiny! Become who you're meant to be. Can't you feel kingship in your veins? You're marvelous. Greatness is who you are. Greatness is who your children are and will be. Your children are the greatest gift you will ever have as a result of being co-creators with God. Stay out of jail and prison.

Forgive

Son or daughter if your father doesn't come to comfort you
wipe away your tears and as your father lives
when he needs you....do forgive.

CHAPTER 8

IT'S NOT "ALL" ABOUT THE "CHILD/CHILDREN'S" MOTHER

At the end of the day the standard is "What is in the best interest of the child". Some women try to set the standard as "you can't see the kids or be in the children's life without me". No, that is not the TRUTH! Don't settle for the lie. Stay in the relationship if you can stay to preserve the unity of the family; but, leave if you must leave to preserve your sanity and maintain constant love for your children. You're still going to be the same father to your children with or without the mother.

Perhaps the mother perceives herself as your family; but, the truth is........... your kids are your family when you're not married. It takes courage to know when a relationship is over. This is a subject where you and you alone in this particular matter must do some soul searching. Is this relationship positive or negative for me? Do I love this woman? Are our goals and dreams compatible?

Many people have an idea about how things should be; but, a lot of times things just do not turn out to be that way. There's fantasy and then there's reality. People have to learn to make their own dreams come true. You can't be their total dream. You have your dreams and that person has theirs and the two must fit to make a whole.

Once, you have kids....(yes, perhaps marriage should have come first) together, then you really know that person and sometimes, that's when you really realize that this is not the person I want to spend the rest of my life with. Well, darn. So should you stay in an unhappy relationship? Where you try to force yourself to be happy because of the children?

No, you should cut your losses, make a clean break, and be totally honest with yourself and the mother. Do not continue to lead her on by making false promises. Are you being honest? Are you being fair? When you hurt the mother you inadvertently hurt the children. People can't focus right and make the best choices for themselves or their children when they are in "heartbreak" pain. So, man up!

Sometimes human beings can be very selfish and just don't want the other person to be with anybody else if they are not with them. At the same time knowing that the relationship is over. Life, just doesn't work that way. As painful as a breakup is at some point we must stand up and face the music. It's never acceptable nor understandable why in the general sense a mother will not allow the father to see the kids just because their relationship is over. But, I love him! Sometimes, love as great and grand as it is......is not enough. We've been lied to in many ways. We have been sold the Cinderella story and therefore, reality is hard to face.

Unhealthy relationships are not in the best interest of children. Constant fussing, cursing, and fighting in front of the kids is ridiculous; actually it is a form of child cruelty. Especially, when the police becomes involved. Maturity is coming to the realization and acknowledging that "Hey we can't get along". Our dreams, goals, and lifestyles are quite different and no matter how much we try....... we just keep butting heads. Something has to change.

Within that change, don't let go of your children. Keep them at the forefront of your heart. Let nothing or no one come between you and your love for your children, not even their mother. Remember, that you don't have to fight and argue physically for your rights to be a father. That's what the courts are for. Simply, go to court and fight for your rights on paper by following the legal process that is already provided for you. Never let a woman dangle your children in front of your face like a toy. Ask for your legal rights and when they are granted be responsible. If you're not going to be responsible, then do nothing. Be true to yourself.

Both men and women of today seek to turn their boy/girlfriends, wives or husbands against mothers and fathers. Why? Where did this evil come from?

During a recent conversation with an older mother, she stated that she doesn't understand "these women these days" they act as if they don't want sons doing anything for their mothers!" Back in my day, daughter-in-laws became daughters and son-in-laws became sons.

Many women today are so self centered that they hate the man's mother before the relationship begins. Why? Evil...they are from their father...the devil. They don't care that the son loves his mother out of pure love. They only care about what that man can do for them and them only. It doesn't matter that the son and mother remembers the struggles and sacrifices that the mother made to raise the child for success. Wow!

Many women will laugh and make jokes regarding the love that the son has for his mother, "Oh, he's a mama's boy!" Only in their deception do they say these things. It is a deception of control. It is an evil game that they play. They are trying to say that you are less than a man! Wow! How is it that you're only a man if they say that you're a man? That really doesn't make any sense. You've already been raised and is a man regardless of what anybody says!

First, you are men because: God determined you to be a man! Secondly, you're a man because they know from their physical experience with you that you are all man. They are NOT confused!
Why, would someone want to come into someone else's family and break it up? Why, not come in and become a loving part of the family?

These are the same women that will conveniently forget the scripture that forbids fornication (sex before marriage) and cry...(quoting holy) scripture about how a man shall leave his mother and father and cleave unto his wife. If all the things in the world were perfect then that would be true for us today; however, that scripture is for a normal household where the mother and father are still living together as husband and wife.

I have learned a valuable lesson and I give it to you."Do not quote scripture if you're not going to live by scripture!" That is a grave sin. Let's not pretend that we love God's word when we don't.

People must rightly divide the word of God. Everyone has a place. Whatever you do, do not take advice from just anybody. Be extremely careful, from where you get your advice from.

Another one of the lies that our society tells us is that our children must always decide for themselves whom they will marry. That's not true. One must do his due diligence to find someone that will "fit" in their family. One should study as to why "India" has such a high marital success rate.

Your mother should have an influence on who you marry! Yes. Why, because, we're women ourselves! Need I say more? We can "see". Please note that there is an exception to every rule.

Don't ever forget your mother. If you can afford to buy your mother a house or in any way make her life more comfortable...do it. You only have one mother.

Most importantly, love. Don't break up your relationship with your mother/parents. If you barbecued with your family every Saturday before your new relationship, barbecue every other Saturday. Keep family relationships strong. There is enough love and a place in your heart for everybody.

Choose the right woman to marry. I tread lightly on this subject. Most of the time your mama knows what's best for you. Always has. (With a few exceptions of course) You have to choose the right woman to be a part of your family and also the right stepmother for your children. Choosing the wrong woman can destroy you both mentally, physically, and financially; the wrong partner can keep you from growing and reaching your full potential/destiny.

If many black men would be honest they would tell you that "Man, I should have listened to my mama!"

Mothers want their children to marry. First, of all there is nothing like real love. Everyone should experience that. Secondly, there is nothing better than grandbabies! Ha! Ha!

Don't let nobody change who you are. Relationships are supposed to add to our lives. Use common sense. Be fair. Be moral. Be kind.

CHAPTER 9

REQUITE YOUR PARENTS

Men you teach your children how to treat you later on in life, by the way that you treat your parents right now; especially, in the case of a single mother who raised you alone.

Between 70 and 72% of all black households are headed by single mothers.

According to an online study of the word "requite" it is defined as: to make appropriate return for (a favor, service, or wrongdoing). Requite also means to respond to (love or affection); return. Return to your mother or father the love that was given to you as a child up to adulthood.

We have been misdirected here in America. The lies and half-truths of our society have torn us from where we originally started. In the beginning we had love and respect for our parents just as God told us to do. We honored our parents. We honored our elders. We must go back to that place of sanity. We must return to the nucleus of our soul. That nucleus is Love. Love for all. Our mothers who worked so hard to raise us alone, deserves nothing but the best from us.

The love from our parents is pure no strings attached. We must remember the love that is like the love of "God" that has been given to us since our birth. This love is unconditional.

First, of all families have always lived together and still do. Look around you. Hence, goes the old proverb "the family that stays together prays together" and "together we stand and divided we fall". Let's read 1 Timothy 5:4 (KJV) "[4] But if any widow have children or nephews, let them learn first to shew piety at home, and to requite their parents: for that is good and acceptable before God. This is something that pleases God.

No, many single mothers are not widowed within the definition of the word "widow"; but, has been left alone to raise their children as if the man was already dead. It is extremely hard. Therefore, when these children become adults, then it is right and just for them to stay at home, get a job, and continue being a family as they have always done all of their lives. There is nothing wrong with being good to your parents/parent.

CHAPTER 10

RAISE YOUR NEPHEWS AND NIECES

I know you think that I have lost my mind. No, I remember my mother telling me that for the most part, her Uncle raised her. Oh, how she loved that man because he first loved her.

My father used to say, “Life is a ball game and everybody must play”! You see the game of life goes something like this. Your nieces and nephews are part of your “family” team and like it or not they are in the dugout, on the field, in the lockers, and at home with you. Reach one teach one. Because, they too may be fatherless and not have their father around daily. Treat these children as your own.

When you’re up there batting at home play, please believe they are cheering for you right along with your own children! They are praying that you hit a home run by getting that new job or promotion. The children hope that you accomplish all your dreams because you’re the only one right now that they have to look up to and you’re planting that seed of love and success within them. At some point the children realize that you’re both from the same blood.

They will someday carry on what you’ve started. One day they will be at home plate batting and you will be sitting in the stands or dugout of life. They will remember you with great love and admiration. You see you cannot plant the great seed of love and it not come back to you in abundance.

So, make sure that whenever you can, support these kids by going to their schools to check on them, clothes, shoes, food, and whatever else they may need. Think of them as your own children. Don't play the role of being a good step father to another man's child and forget about your own blood ties. Be a good uncle and a good stepfather. You can be both. Maybe not always at the same time; but, you can do it. As a matter of fact, be good to all children that you come into contact with.

CHAPTER 11

SAVE YOUR MONEY

Learn how to save money. Good credit is fine; but, cash in savings or cd is better to me. You should always do your best to put money aside so that you can have some money to fall back on.

If you don't have a savings account today, go out and get one. One hundred dollars a month in savings will be twelve hundred dollars in twelve months. If you can't do that, just save what you can.

How will your children have a chance to go to college without a head start in life from you? You should start your children a college fund right now.

Financial Management consists of:

1. Studying financial management.
2. Learning how to invest and what to invest in.
3. Consultation with a financial advisor.
4. Networking with people with money.

BLACK MAN'S GUIDE TO FULFILLING YOUR DESTINY!

Self-Improvement/Goal Setting

by

Linda D. Crowder

Introduction

Do you know who you are? You should renew your search for "Black History. Many things that we have been taught in America are lies; especially, history. You will find out that you're a descendant of Kings and Queens. Find out about the good, the bad, and the ugly. Some of this information will give you a sense of pride. Some of this information will leave you with questions that only God can answer. Open your eyes and began to see out of the "eye" of knowledge. You must teach your children to "see".

You must ask yourself:

1. "Where was the beginning of humankind"?
2. "Where were the oldest bones found known to man"?
3. "How does all this relate to me and who I am inside"?

The goal of this workbook is for you to become motivated and focused on yourself and your dreams. What do you want out of life and how will you get what you want? This is what's called self-determination and self-inspiration.

You must reach within yourself to pull out all that is there to fulfill your destiny!

Day 1

Affirmation

Affirm your faith. Who and what do you believe in as this belief relates to God? (For an example: Christianity, Judaism, Mormons, etc.)

1. I believe in the following:

____
____
____
____
____
____
____
____
____
____
____

2. I will began or continue to pray every morning: (What will you pray about or who will you pray for?)

____
____
____
____
____
____
____
____
____
____

Day 2

Goal Setting

What is it that you would like to accomplish? (For example: new job, business owner.)

1. I would like to:

 ____
 ____
 ____
 ____
 ____
 ____
 ____
 ____
 ____
 ____
 ____

2. What short-term goals will you set as a start for reaching your goal? (Example: Buy newspaper to look for job, surf the internet every day.)

 ____
 ____
 ____
 ____
 ____
 ____
 ____
 ____
 ____
 ____

Day 3

Keep Your Eyes on the Prize

Plan to remain focused on what you're going to accomplish: (Example: Buying a calendar or keeping a log of job search)

1. I will remain focused on my goals by doing the following:

____
____
____
____
____
____
____
____
____
____
____
____
____
____
____
____
____
____
____
____
____

Day 4

Getting the Proper Sleep, Food, & Exercise

What will you do to get the proper sleep, food/healthy eating, and exercise? (For an example: I will go to bed earlier, buy more fresh foods, and develop my own exercise routine.)

1. To get the proper sleep: I will.....

   ____
   ____
   ____
   ____
   ____
   ____
   ____
   ____
   ____
   ____
   ____

2. Proper Food/Healthy eating: I will.....

   ____
   ____
   ____
   ____
   ____
   ____
   ____
   ____
   ____
   ____

3. Proper Exercise: I will.....

Day 5

Make Savings a Top-Priority- Avoid Debt

What will you do to save money? What will you do to avoid debt? (For an example: I will open a savings account and put money in it every payday, spend less on unnecessary habits, to avoid debt...make cash purchases only.)

1. To save money: I will.....

   ____
   ____
   ____
   ____
   ____
   ____
   ____
   ____
   ____
   ____
   ____

2. To cut spending on unnecessary items: I will.....

   ____
   ____
   ____
   ____
   ____
   ____
   ____
   ____
   ____
   ____

3. To avoid debt: I will.....

Day 6

Overcome Negative Thinking

What will you do to overcome negative thinking? (For an example: I will reaffirm my faith by reading the Bible everyday and pray or I will buy a self-improvement book/positive thinking book.)

1. I will overcome negative thinking by:
____
____
____
____
____
____
____
____
____
____
____
____
____
____
____
____
____
____
____
____
____

Day 7

Know Who Your Friends Are: Build Your Team of Life

Knowing who your friends are is a key element to your success. Some people are placed in your life to elevate you. Know who those key players are. Stop wasting your time with people who don't mean you any good or who have no plans for success. The wrong friends can choke your motivation and stifle your growth. Do not accept advice from just anybody no matter how successful or unsuccessful they are. Because a person is successful in a certain venue does not mean that he or she has the right answer for your life. (For an example: I will choose friends that want something out of life.)

1. To choose my life team: I will.....

 ____
 ____
 ____
 ____
 ____
 ____
 ____
 ____
 ____
 ____
 ____
 ____
 ____
 ____
 ____

Day 8

Manage Your Time- Organize Your Life

What will you do to manage your time; because managing your time means organizing your life! (For an example: Research time management tips.)

1. To manage my time: I will.....

Day 9

Meditate 10-15 Minutes a Day

Get in a quiet place and meditate for ten minutes.

1. What are your thoughts?

2. What creative ideas did you receive?

3. What will you do to make these creative ideas a reality? What simple steps will you use to reach your divine goals?

Day 10

Be Good To Yourself

Sometimes we're always running and doing for others. Stop for a minute. Be good to yourself. Take yourself out to dinner. Go see a movie. Make sure that you get some "me" time in every week.

1. I will be good to myself by doing the following:

Day 11

Make A Dream Poster

Make a dream poster containing all the things you want to accomplish or have. (For an example: Well rounded kids...you can place pictures of you and the kids...at church, a park, at school, doing homework, going shopping, nice house, car, whether you want to be an author, business owner, singer, dancer, etc.) Let your mind run wild!

1. To make my "Dream" poster: I will.....

Day 12

Learn a New Skill

There are many short term courses that in the long term offers a good salary; such as taxes, painting, and landscaping. Just beware of online education scams. Contact local schools and colleges or a listing of "Continuing Education Courses". So learn a new skill or brush up on old skills.

1. To learn a new skill: I will.....

____
____
____
____
____
____
____
____
____
____
____
____
____
____
____
____
____
____
____
____
____

Day 13

Do Away With Expensive Over Indulgent Habits!

Whether, your habit is chocolates or chips, beer or cigarettes........let go! Take that money and put it into your new savings account. Yea! Write down what you're willing to let go.

1. To do away with expensive habits: I will.....

____
____
____
____
____
____
____
____
____
____
____
____
____
____
____
____
____
____
____
____
____

Day 14

Respect People!

Respect others and how they feel about things. Respect their culture and always recognize that we're all a part of the human race. No one person is any better than the other person. We can always think better and make better decisions; but, we're no better on the human level.

1. To respect others: I will.....

Day 15

Plant Something!

Plant something simple or grow a big garden! It really doesn't matter. Drop a corn or onion seed in fertilized soil and watch the amazing miracle working power of the Almighty! There's just something about putting the seed in the ground, where you know that the seed will die; but, will produce something beautiful of the same.

1. To plant something beautiful: I will.....

Day 16

Plan to travel!

Make future travel plans for yourself and for your family. Traveling opens your eyes to life and gets you out of "your" box. Many times we only see life as our environment; but, when we change that environment then we can see the big picture. Your trip doesn't have to be long. It can be for the weekend.

1. To make travel plans: I will.....

Day 17

Visualize!

Visualize what you want in life. See your children in college after all of the homework, good and tough times you've had raising them. See yourself in that new car or house. Visualize, visualize, visualize!

1. In my vision, I see:

____
____
____
____
____
____
____
____
____
____
____
____
____
____
____
____
____
____
____
____
____

Day 18

Love and Reverence God!

Fearing God is interpreted as respecting Him and His commandments.

1. To fear God: I will.....

____
____
____
____
____
____
____
____
____
____
____
____
____
____
____
____
____
____
____
____
____
____
____
____

Day 19

Maintain Good Work Ethics!

Maintain good work ethics. You never know who is watching you and where your good habits will lead you.

1. To maintain good work ethics: I will.....

Day 20

Keep Your Entrepreneurship Spirit!

Keep in mind that some people will never grow rich by working on someone else's job. Always think and dream of having your own business part-time or full-time. You can have your own business in addition to the job that you currently have. You can sell T-Shirts, food plates, books, water, etc. The sky is the limit! Own your own business! You can start an internet company. Do the research! Find or create digital or e-book products to sell all around the world.

1. To keep my Entrepreneurship Spirit: I will.....

____

____

____

____

____

____

____

____

____

____

____

____

____

____

____

____

____

____

____

Day 21

Recognize the Miracles Around You!

Count your blessings one by one.

1. I am thankful for the following:

Day 22

Love Even When Loving Is Not Easy!

Some relationships are nothing but torture; let go if you have to! What is wrong with you? Make sure you're fair in your assessment. Let the person or persons know what you like or dislike regarding the relationship; if change is impossible....then let go.

Some family members have to be loved from a distance. Don't stop loving just love from a distance. If a situation occurs and you can help the person...help them; but, you're not required to pick them up forever.

No matter what, YOU know when you're in a bad relationship. Grow up and get the hell out!

1. To love even when loving is not easy: I will.....

____

____

____

____

____

____

____

____

____

____

____

____

____

____

____

Day 23

Positive Thinking!

Develop the habit of thinking positive. Think....I can! Exhibit a positive attitude that will flow from you to others.

1. To keep a positive attitude: I will.....

Day 24

Spend Time With Family!

Spend quality time with your family. Time gone is time that you cannot get back. If you have an argument, cool off and start all over. Life is too short for such hostility. (For an example: Plan a picnic, a day at the park, or theme park.)

1. To spend quality time with family: I will.....

Day 25

Monitor And Manage Your Thoughts!

Most of the time if you have happy thoughts, you will have happy conversations; keeps your thoughts happy. Don't watch the news every day. Monitor and manage your thoughts. Have you noticed that there have been times when you were thinking something and mistakenly said exactly what you were thinking? Wow!

1. To monitor and manage my thoughts: I will.....

____
____
____
____
____
____
____
____
____
____
____
____
____
____
____
____
____
____
____
____
____

Day 26

Laugh, Don't Forget To Laugh!

Laughter is medicine to our souls. Laugh at the silly things of life because this is what gets us through life. Find a "joke" website. Talk to an old friend.....and just laugh!

1. I will laugh at silly things such as:

Day 27

Don't Forget To Cry!

One of the biggest lies that has ever been told is that men aren't supposed to cry. Crying is a cleanser of the heart; perhaps, the very opposite of laughing. In your time of sorrow you must let that which is natural happen naturally so that you can began to heal. You DO NOT have to be ashamed. Real men cry when they feel real pain/sorrow.

1. I will remember that crying is a healer too!

Day 28

Be Faithful and Committed in Your "Love" Relationships!

Most of the time if you stay faithful and committed to one person you will have fewer problems. Fewer worries about STDs if you got yourself checked out before the current relationship began. There are exceptions to every rule. The general rule is that there is trust in a faithful committed relationship.

1. To be faithful and committed: I will.....

____
____
____
____
____
____
____
____
____
____
____
____
____
____
____
____
____
____
____
____
____

Day 29

Get Knowledge!

Seek out and obtain knowledge. Know yourself. There are many academic resources on Black History. Just Google or YouTube the following phrases:

"Black History Academic Resources".
"They Came Before Columbus"
"The Foods We Eat"

After you have learned black history, then learn world history, state history, city history, etc. There are a lot of free audio and e-books online. There are a lot of free university and foreign language podcasts.

1. To seek out and obtain knowledge: I will.....

____
____
____
____
____
____
____
____
____
____
____
____
____
____
____
____

Day 30

Discover the Power Within You!

Discover the creative abilities within you. What do you do best? What makes you a great person? What are your weaknesses and how can you turn your weaknesses into strengths? What are your strengths? How can you turn your strengths into power that will help you accomplish your goals? For example: If you're a singer, then will you create a singing YouTube video to get you started on your way to earning **$$$** or either just for the fun of doing a video?

1. To discover the power within me: I will.....

____
____
____
____
____
____
____
____
____
____
____
____
____
____
____
____
____
____
____

About the Author:

Name: Linda D. Crowder
Country: United States
Contact: crowder807@yahoo.com
Blog: ladyctalks.blogspot.com
Hobbies: Reading, Writing, Cookbooks.

www.ingramcontent.com/pod-product-compliance
Lightning Source LLC
LaVergne TN
LVHW051815080426
835513LV00017B/1969

* 9 7 8 0 6 1 5 9 4 0 7 8 6 *